It was raining, and Gregory was feeling grumpy.

'Shall we go for a little walk?' said Sue.

But on the way out, Gregory fell down and hurt his knee!

Gregory and Marta came back
inside to play.

Then at snack time, Gregory only got one piece of red apple.

After snack time, it was raining even harder.

Gregory and Marta couldn't play in the sand.

At home time, Gregory still felt grumpy.
'I've had a grumpy day,' he said.

Sometimes
I have a bad
day too.

'Yippee!' said Marta.

Gregory's Grumpy Day

Introduction

This story is about Gregory, a little boy who sometimes has trouble coping with the little problems and challenges he meets during the day. The problems seem to mount up through the morning at his childminder's, until his mum arrives and explains that she feels grumpy sometimes too, and suggests a favourite outing to cheer him up!

Top tips for using this book

Remember that you don't need to do them all at once!

1 Feeling 'grumpy' can result from tiredness, frustration or hunger, and Gregory seems to suffer from all three! Read the book together, and talk about how Gregory feels, and about how his friend Marta responds to his feelings. Empathy - understanding how others feel - is an important step on the way to managing the same feelings yourself. Talk about what Gregory could do in each situation to cheer himself up. Give your child time to think, and if he or she can't think of anything, suggest something yourself.

2 Play a game where you try to think of lots of feelings, such as happy, sad, tired, grumpy, excited, cross, or frustrated. Make the face as you say the feeling. Ask your child if s/he can feel his/her body change when they make an angry face or a surprised face. Try playing this game sitting next to each other in front of a mirror.

3 Recognising emotions on other people's faces is an important part of understanding feelings. Make a simple little book, using a long strip of paper folded in a zigzag. Draw a circle on each page and help your child draw different eyes and mouths to make each face have a different expression. A mirror may help you to talk about the way faces change to show how you feel.

4 If your child feels grumpy at the beginning of the day, talk about what is making them feel grumpy. Perhaps they need something to eat, a rest, or a distraction. The important thing is that your child can begin to recognise the feeling for him/herself.

5 Make a game by sticking pictures or drawings of faces on pieces of card. Use these to play a 'Name the Feeling' game. Put the cards face down on the floor and turn them over one at a time, naming the feelings. You could make two of each card to play a matching game.

6 Use a teddy or other favourite soft toy to help your child think about changing feelings. Say: 'Teddy's feeling cross because he wants to play outside and it's raining. Can you make him feel better?' Give your child time to think, and take all their suggestions seriously. Remember that children sometimes have very different ideas from adults!

Published 2014 by Featherstone Education
An imprint of Bloomsbury Publishing Plc
50 Bedford Square, London, WC1B 3DP
www.bloomsbury.com

Bloomsbury is a registered trademark of Bloomsbury Publishing Plc

ISBN 978-1-4729-0772-1

Text © Nicola Call and Sally Featherstone
Illustrations © Melissa Four

A CIP record for this publication is available from
the British Library.

Printed in China by Leo Paper Products, Heshan, Guangdong

This book is produced using paper that is made
from wood grown in managed, sustainable forests.
It is natural, renewable and recyclable. The logging
and manufacturing process conform to the environmental
regulations of the country of origin.

10 9 8 7 6 5 4 3 2 1